Where I Sit

Also by Donald Lev

A Very Funny Fellow
Wings - 20 Poems of Devotion
The Darkness Above: Selected Poems 1968-2002
Yesterday's News
Enemies of Time
Twilight
There Is Still Time
Twentieth Century Limited
Intercourse with the Dead
Peculiar Merriment
Hyn and Other Poems

Where I Sit

poems by

Donald Lev

PRESA PRESS
ROCKFORD, MI

Copyright © 2015 Donald Lev

All rights reserved. No part of this book may be reproduced in any manner whatsoever, without the express written consent of the publisher, except in the case of brief excerpts in critical reviews and articles. All inquiries should be addressed to: Presa Press, P.O. Box 792, Rockford, Michigan 49341.

Acknowledgments

Some of the poems in this book originally appeared in the following **Magazines**: *Big Hammer, Chiron Review, Heliotrope, Home Planet News Online, House Organ, Lips, Street Value, Waterways, Waymark* and *Waywayanda Review;* **Books**: *The Art of Survival - An Anthology* (Kings Estate Press), *At The Gate: Departures and Arrivals* (Kings Estate Press) and *The Brownstone Poets 2013 Anthology* (Brownstone Poets).
Cover art "Red Wine" by Lora Shelley.

First Edition

Printed in the United States of America

ISBN: 978-0-9888279-9-8

Library of Congress Control Number: 2014956779

Cataloging Information: 1. Lev, Donald, 1936- ;
2. Contemporary American Poetry

PRESA PRESS
PO Box 792   Rockford, MI 49341
presapress@aol.com   presapress@aol.com

Where I Sit

"You see the world from where you sit."
　　　Mary Lev (the author's mother)

Contents

I. INITIATION

Initiation..11
The Meeting...12
In Lower Manhattan................................13
Dover Beach: A Minute Contemplation......14
Today's Poem...15
The Bear..16
A Poem For Putin....................................17
Good Work...18
One Brick At A Time...............................19
I Think It Was A Bus...............................20
Last Wine Tasting...................................21
Bimini...22
Operation..23
Blood..24
Spring Has Come....................................25
Poem For Poetry Month.........................26
April 12th, 1945......................................27
BB...28
Jazz Lyric..29
A Martini On Maundy Thursday............30
I Have A Vision......................................32
To Horse!..33
Exchanges..34
History..35
Skype...36
Straining..37
As Anyone Could See.............................38
Caveat..39
Naggings..40
The Binding Of Isaac..............................41
The Aviator's Tale...................................42
The Tingling...43
My Half-Brother And I...........................44
Union Square...45
All Art..46
At Sea..47
Cento...48

II. ENUMERATION

A Poverty 51
An Island 52
The Art Of Suggestion 53
A Box Of Sand 54
Beefeater At The Gate 55
Destiny 56
Fourth Of July Meditation 57
From The Forbidden Apocrypha 58
Root Juices 59
Cocktail Hour, Snug's, New Paltz 60
Washington Park, Albany 61
The Lesson 62
Pride 63
Loyalty 64
The Chatter 65
Hitler 66
Jacks 67
Moment Of Hollywood History 68
Aesthetic 69
How The West Is Being Won 70
On The Film, *Once* 71
"Am I The Kind Of Girl You Take To Blimpies?" 72
Crow 73
Postscript 74
Progress Report 75
Stadium 76
The Day 77
Man's Grandeur 78
Abandonment 79
In Memoriam 80
Apples 81
Let's Take A Look 82
Good King Ludwig 83
Definition 84
Götterdämmerung 85
Poem In Late October 86
Author's Bio 87

INITIATION

Initiation

An ant exploring a new surface
Anxious for footing
Secure enough to avoid
The shoe poised above him:
That's me, composing, for the first time,
A poem on a personal computer.

A computer that seems to insist
On initial capitals.

The Meeting

There was a meeting
In an old brick building,
On the third floor, I guess.
A freight elevator helped
You to the floor,
But you couldn't get there
Too late.

The agenda for the evening was set by,
I forget who, but no matter.
Much time has passed,
And some very few of us are still present.

In Lower Manhattan

In Lower Manhattan, somewhere,
Maybe the Marc Ballroom,
The Flatiron Building,
Or that place between

Fourth Avenue and Third Avenue
Before it was a rock 'n-roll club

I saw Pete Seeger's head
Disappear in light,
in *fervent* light.

A miraculous vision
I wish now to report
This day after the
Saint has been carried away.

1/28/14

Dover Beach: A Minute Contemplation

". . .gleams, and is gone. . ."
Is all my soul's content just this moment.

Today's Poem

. . .finds me walking on ice,
Hoping I have no reason to run.

The Bear

This bear
Came walking down the path
Leading into my backyard.

He had a plastic bracelet from some
Hospital around his wrist
And I could see he
Looked worried,
And not quite sure where he was going.

Still I ran back into the house
And went looking for my shotgun
Because that is what you do
When you see a bear
In your back yard.

A Poem For Putin

"O the Soviet Union just keeps rolling along"
Sang one of the folkniks at one of the Yale Hoots back in
 '56 or '57,
Which, like the Pepsi Cola jingle I can't get out of my
 Head.

It's not politics, well, not exactly.
I do miss the cold war, its philosophical possibilities,

But I can always watch my old Star Trek videos for that.

Good Work

First of all, it's awlmanac, not aaalmanac, stoopid.
But Garrison, I am so grateful
That you remembered
Mickey Spillane's birthday!

One Brick At A Time

That's how I chose to go about things.
There was this construction site
With more bricks than they knew what to do with,
So every night I'd help myself to a brick or two,
Which, in my much abused used wheel-barrow,
I'd wheel over to my site.
As you can well imagine,
Nothing much ever came of this,
At least as far as I was concerned.

The other project, a shopping mall, was built.
I'm still working on mine.

I Think It Was A Bus

I think it was a bus
I was waiting for
When I began waiting.

Now I'm not so sure,
But odds are that was a bus.
Now I'm just waiting.

Last Wine Tasting

Overcast with shades of Malbee
Redolent of dirty wars
And disappearances...

I cut my finger slicing cheese
And beat a prudent retreat
With a Rioja,

Tasting of salt, blood, history.

Bimini

Salt spray so refreshing
As the small boat cut east
Toward an island waiting
Like a parting in the sea
For troubled footsteps
Fleeing not
Speedily enough.

Operation

They wheeled me in front of the large desk.
I was asked my name.
I replied guilty.
That apparently was the answer they were seeking,
So, the procedure proceeded.
The outcome is to be conveyed in the beak of a pigeon.

Blood

"Here's blood in yer eye," he quipped,
And recited his latest update of "America.."

I broke into a chorus
Of "Yankee Doodle Dandy," I don't know why.
Just felt like being silly I guess.

Spring Has Come

Spring has come
With a lot of wind and sun
And rain.
Pain, too,
To rhyme with rain.

Not that I needed the rhyme. I just
Wanted it.

Poem For Poetry Month

April is the wettest month;
Cruel, maybe, too.

But it's only Time.

April 12th, 1945

President Franklin Delano Roosevelt died.
At the age of nine,
I had known no other President.
I had not yet conceived
Of the phenomenon called death.
I was listening to the radio, to
"Daniel Boone on Wilderness Road"
When it was interrupted with the news.

I thought I'd tell you this.

BB

The Seatons, Bill and Patricia
(The last of the Flower Children)
Once cascaded upon me
All their home videos they made
Of their many years of
Quality tv watching,
Because I was one of the last to
Acquire and enjoy good old fashioned VHS videos.
Well after a long while that my
Old tv (my video monitor since clearing entirely to
    High Falls
Some years ago)
Was repaired, thanks to Phil Levine, actor, poet, and
    decent poetry reading series host,
I began watching the Seaton Tapes.
BB King. My esthetics rearranged themselves forever.
Ask me for a definition of The Beautiful, I would not
    hesitate to
Reply BB King .
Shaped like a
minotaur with a guitar,
what control!

Gladys Knight– how beautiful– Etta James, Albert King,
Some great honkies, Eric Clapton, Dr. John–
But BB is smooth in control.
And when he ordains: "let the good times roll"
Even a morukh like me
Manages a wee rock if not a total roll.

Jazz Lyric

I'm at the end of my rope and I'm
Swingin'

A Martini On Maundy Thursday

I'd just managed to stumble over to the tavern
After my podiatrist appointment
And was I thirsty!   They were just
Climbing the stairs and I was
Surprised when they invited me to join them.

Well, *they* didn't.
Just Si, otherwise known as Rocky, who
I used to drink with now and then (Rocky
Was a mindless, garrulous sort and would drink with
 anybody.).
But the others– the hard-working sons of Zebedee,
 with their stone eyes–
Matthew the hustling businessman - - -that weird Judas,
Whose eyes would be wandering all over the place
When he was talking to you– definitely not my scene.

The women were alright, but they only related to the big
 guy, the preacher,
Who was ok, I guess, I never got that up close to him.
He had this kind of fanatic shininess to him–
Charisma I think they call it– which is sort of a turn-off
 to me.
He'd get big crowds at his talks but I was usually
On the edges, out of, or almost out of
Earshot. What I managed to hear wasn't anything
 new,
But I guess he put it over, especially to the kids.
Anyway, people stopped inviting me to their seders
 years ago.
I can't blame them. I'm toothless, have too few changes
 of clothes, and tend
To drink too much wine.

So I told Rocky
I needed to rest my feet, but maybe I'd come up later.
What I really wanted was an ice cold martini
To celebrate the parting of the sea.

And you know we grow the
Best olives in the world in this country.

I Have A Vision

I have a vision to report.
My vision is of God's blindness.
How He hears our prayers, but
Can't tell where they're coming from.
So that may go some way
To explain some of our disappointments.

To Horse!

To horse! Some one shouted in a
Stentorian British accent.

I ran out to see if I could find one,
A horse that is, not a stentorian Briton.
I must have gotten myself into this Shakespearean play.
I thought I was auditioning for something else.
Anyway, when someone handed me a saddle
And a harness to put on the horse
(Oh, did I tell you? a horse appeared!)
I thought that was too much of a day's work
So I quit on the spot
And never returned to the theater.

I'll continue my memoirs in the morning.

Exchanges

In this dream,
Which I wish
I didn't recall,
I confronted the candidate
With the question
"How would you like
A demonstration of democracy?"

After which I turned
And sat upon his face.

I awoke repenting
My decision in college
To exchange my
Political Science major
For one in English.

History

A head filled with history
Will hardly prevent what's to come,
But one must watch where one walks,
Mustn't one?

Skype

Bullets and grenades whizzed past me.
Thank God I lead a charmed life but
This made me pretty nervous.
I was being streamed in to this
Belligerent crowd
Via something they called skype (I think).
I did my usual stuff but they just didn't like me.
It's about time to start
Cutting back on technology,
Don't you think?

Straining

I'm sitting here with a constipated mind
Straining and straining but nothing's coming.
I need a vacation I'm thinking.
By the bright blue Aegean.

At a seaside tavern with my old friend Rudy
And his charming wife Lisi.

We are drinking Ouzo and retsina
Like you can't get here Rudy told me
On his last visit.

We're eating
Some sort of divine herring
Fresh from the sea fried just right
With a little squeeze of lemon.

There's a goddess beckoning
Me from her half shell
But I'm too comfortable to move.

As Anyone Could See

As anyone could see,
I needed a brain transplant.
I needed $5,000 to get one,
So I decided to apply
To New York State via
It's New York Lottery
Scratch off card program
Where you get two chances
To win for two dollars.

An investment of twenty
Should do it, I thought.

Caveat

Many things come out of darkness.
I will call them lights out of ignorance,
But they aren't really.
Rather they are shapes of darkness
That create

Interest in themselves
For those who find interest nowhere else.

Naggings

Birds fly broken-winged
Across twilit family skies
Where generations
Lay weight on one another,
Where mysteries
Grow savage with nightfall.

The Binding Of Isaac

This is my greatest poem, a truly major work.
Expressed here are all the horrors of my life,
Real or imagined, organized as a re-telling
Of the binding of Isaac, with, of course,
The knife being wielded by the mother.

Then there were the two brief spin-offs.
What did I do with them? Clipped them
In a notebook, but what did I do with the notebook?
The spin-offs I need for envoi. My epic
Won't work without them.

Well I'll look for them
In the morning.

I have no intention
Of getting out of bed now.

*I didn't write any
Epic poem.*

I dreamt it. What a relief!

The Aviator's Tale

Flying above the clouds,
I chanced to look down
And saw a big circular hole
In the cloud below me.

I looked more carefully
And saw a similar hole
In the cloud below that one.

On extremely close inspection
Another hole appeared
In the cloud below that one.

That, children,
Was how it was
To fly over Broadway
Before they banned
Cigarette advertizing.

The Tingling

There is a tingling in my left arm
That for some reason or non-reason
I choose to think of as the tingling of hope.

My Half-Brother And I

Funny how
My half-brother and I
Both resemble our mothers
But each of us in ways that seem
Important to us, emulates our father.

Union Square

"Brothers and sisters, sisters and brothers:
You know I sweated blood for this union."
I was impressed and moved, or would have been,
If some of those brothers weren't trying to steer me
By my elbows toward a big window opening onto
East 17th Street.

Our shop steward was being
Brought up on some sort of charges, so some of us
Accompanied him to the meeting to keep an eye on
things.

I have been in good unions and bad unions. And the only
Thing worse than a bad union is no union.

I hope
The above vignette illustrates this, but it probably
doesn't.

All Art

The frame.

I always begin with the frame.
All art is limitation.

At Sea

"I'll sail my ship alone
Tho' all the sails be torn" sang Moon Mullican,
The great country & western piano player.

Here I am, here I'll sit
Waiting for a call-back for my next starring role.

Cento

There's nothing new under the sun.
God bless us all, every one.

ENUMERATION

A Poverty

I sit here
Watching
Things
Go back & forth
Absorbing
Life, the gift thereof.

There are no interactions
That I am part of
That I am aware of.

No, nothing.

I sniff the air
And dream of being
Where?

Venice, in a recent film I've seen
Would be nice.

Or maybe Forest Hills, the rail
Road trestles when the fog gathers about them
Or the old White Tower early mornings
After the bars have closed.

I feel within myself
A poverty

Of which I can give no account.

An Island

I know people with seeds of my being
Came off ships in New York harbor
And proceeded on their way into Manhattan
And other Atlantic and Great Lake ports.

They came from places wherein
Their language was not respected,
Nor their ancient, romantic, heroic,
Almost entirely absurd religion;
Which my seedbearers, as far as my
Researches went, took that not
Entirely seriously.

And so I came to be—
As island, if any man was.

The Art Of Suggestion

A house was set afire here in 1757. You can still
Smell the smoke.

I thanked the tour guide and headed off to
The colorful tavern nearby
To get some lunch.

The smell of smoke still haunts me...

My next tour will be Lourdes.

A Box Of Sand

A box of sand.

That's all it is.
I dug around in it, not exactly expecting
To find treasure, but I thought maybe
An old pot or two, which I can
Certainly use?
But no.

Only sand.

Well, sand, I thought, like silvery sands
Under subtropical moonlight?

Mysterious Sahara sands. . .
The Sands of Time?

At least that?

But no.

Just sand.

A box of sand.

"Mister sandman

send

me

a

dream. . ."

No.
Only sand.

Beefeater At The Gate

I bribed the Beefeater at the gate
With a bottle of orange flavored Stolichnaya
And climbed slowly up the twisting stone stairs
Till I reached the chamber where the doomed
Princess was being held.
She greeted me with momentary
Joy and relief, till she realized
I was but a tourist come to see
The few sights that really interested me.

Destiny

Out of the corner of my
Eye, I espy
Peter Lorre staring out my window.

I imagine the ghost of my black cat
Scratching at my back door.

I pour some bourbon into my mug of tea,
And sit down to write this long poem
About destiny.

Fourth Of July Meditation

Bombs bursting in air.

Of course.

Why not?
Still, who is here who is not glad to be here?
Well,

There's the old countries.

See your bride blown up on your visit to Sicily.
In auld Erin you're too fast and they're too slow
And you're just another Yank.
My land is the Ukraine. How's that
For a laugh.

We got out around the time of the
Kishinev pogrom, and a little before the Beilis trial.

There's Israel, our mythic homeland.
Always powerful.

God met us there.
A friend of mine said once,
"I love America, but Israel's home."
That's how he felt. I respect that.

From The Forbidden Apocrypha

Moses slid down the mountain cursing under his breath
At the weight of the useless stone tablets he got talked
    into delivering.
When he saw everyone partying around that beautiful
Golden calf his face brightened even more than the flank
    of the calf.
Delighted, he smashed the tablets and ran down to join
    the festivities.
"Oh Moses!" cried someone, not understanding.
"What have we done? We are so very sorry!
Maybe you can go back and bring us another set?"

Root Juices

The day Muammar Gaddafi was killed
I drove to the Upstate Theater in Rhinebeck
To see a documentary on Sholem Aleichem,
The great Yiddish writer that hailed from the
Shtetl next to the shtetl my father, his numerous siblings,
And their butcher parents had fled
Just ahead of a great pogrom
To eventually emerge in New Haven, Connecticut.
Thus thoroughly soaked in root juices,
Leaving the theater, I passed in the lobby,
A woman exclaiming how she had not realized
The Upstate housed two theaters and she had mistakenly
Sat through the entire Sholem Aleichem film.

Asked whether she enjoyed it, she shook her head
And said she was just puzzled.
Today President Obama declared the Iraq War at an end.

Cocktail Hour, Snug's, New Paltz

Soccer both screens?
Might be anywhere in the world!

I have mourned European colonialism,
The typewriter, and the Cold War.

Is it too early to
Mourn

American Exceptionalism?

Washington Park, Albany

Robert Burns' statue stared straight ahead
Ignoring the poetry reading,
Whose strange dialects and barbaric vocabularies
Invaded the peace 'round his ancient pedestal.

It was Bastille Day. One would have thought
A rebel like Bobbie Burns would be in better spirits.
But the nearby statue of Lawgiver Moses
Celebrated the occasion more dramatically:
Waving his serpent rod over some virtual Red Sea,
And swinging flying banners all over the place,
In a true frenzy of liberation.

7/14/12

The Lesson

The scowling teacher in his
Wrinkled brown suit
Stooped to pick up the eraser
That had just been hurled at him
By an anonymous member of his history class.

He stared menacingly at the class,
His features all at once becoming skeletal.

"O Teacher Death," cried Allen in the back row.
"It wasn't me, it wasn't me!"
As the teacher, Mr. Dunn, steadied
His malignant gaze, then proceeded
To drag young Allen off by the ear.

Pride

I stood still on that spot,
My legs having turned to stone.

My feet felt nothing under them.
And my arms and shoulders
Began to stiffen.

But my brain,
As yet relatively unhardened,
Began wishing for a pedestal.

Loyalty

I named the kitten my neighbor
Had shamed me into adopting
Charlie, after Charles Manson.

He was a cute, cuddly, furry little guy
But I knew better. Cats are sinister.
A little like women, but totally
Unlike men and dogs, they inhabit
Two worlds equally, the wild and the domestic,
With equal loyalty.

They can't be trusted.

The Chatter

I could hear this mumbling
Everywhere, swimming under
Other sound as if under water.

I discerned no clear word, nor even syllable,
Yet the murmuring was in English.
How could it not be?
It wasn't about me. After all, I'm
Not as paranoid as I used to be.

Hitler

It is uncanny
And not a little alarming
To notice how similar in spirit
We are, or were, or are:
Both of us truants,
Late risers,
Lazy,
Both of us preferring
Our own ideas about things
To things.

Neither of us should ever have been trusted
With a country to govern.

Jacks

Hey, Sport!
I lifted my head and looked toward the
Space the voice was coming from,
My jacks forgotten for the moment.

There being no repetition, I returned to my game.
It was serious, after all.
Olympic Jacks.

An ocean nearby was crashing upon a rocky shore
And judgment was being passed, and many condemned.
Rottenness grew at the heart of most things,
But not Olympic Jacks, by God. Not Olympic Jacks.

Moment Of Hollywood History

Did I ever tell you about the time
I woke up and found myself on this funny boat
In the middle of the ocean
And this big party was going on
Girls in exotic costumes
Lots of booze, animals, and Roman soldiers
It was pre code Cecile B. DeMille and I
Found myself on a couch between Fred MacMurray and
Claudette Colbert, and it was my job to introduce them
But I'd forgotten their names.
Meanwhile, the code took effect so everyone
Put their clothes on and Fred and Claudette
Introduced themselves.

Aesthetic

Her dress dropped to the floor. Her
Back was beautiful.
But there were no scars.
She lied about the scars.
I was deputized to shoot her. *Me.*
Fortunately,
The war ended
Abruptly.

There was music.
Credits rolled.

A bird,
Stranded in the north one winter,
Almost froze.

How The West Is Being Won

The dentist retired early (he
Happened to have hit a
Lotto jackpot) and moved to
Arizona– a beautiful country if you
Have all your papers in order– for his
Health; but the bad cough he'd developed
Spending too much time in his
Cigar smoking club back in
New Jersey, would not go away.
His girl friend, who used to be his
Dental assistant,
Wouldn't stop nagging him to at
Least stop smoking, so he
Beat up on her. This is about where
He runs into Wyatt Earp, and you
Pretty much know the rest, except
They never tell you how many
Innocent bystanders got caught
In the cross-fire that legendary
Morning down in the
Oh Kay Shopping Center.

On The Film, *Once*

Boy with guitar on his back meets girl pulling vacuum
   cleaner.
They fall in love, then split, but not before they make their
   music.
(She, it turns out, plays the piano.)
A musical– a bit more subdued than the ones with
Dan Dailey & Betty Grable & Carmen Miranda &
Cuddles Sakall cleaning breadcrumbs off a checkered
Tablecloth- nothing like that.

The music's a bit contemporary for my taste,
Though it begins to grow on me (one number in particular,
That I don't know the name of)...but the theme is there...
Expressed purely: Love & Music & Youth.

Hooray!

"Am I The Kind Of Girl You Take To Blimpies?"

She wasn't.
I guess I was what you call clueless.
I still am.
A long, clueless life.

That's my boast.

Crow

Crows have been flying southward in mobs.
I am one of them, just tailing along
In the wake made powerful by the rest of them;
Trying to mind my own business,
Play with my own thoughts in my
Own mind.

No wonder
My fellow crows don't think much of me.

There's a field I'd like to drop down to,
Rest awhile, beak some corn, and, you know,
Speak words of wisdom to the unheeding.

Postscript

I opened my eyes and stared
Into this blank page
Which should have had a poem on it

Concerning this buoyant old woman
I picture bent double,
Grimacing or smiling, radiantly.
She is wearing a huge gown full of big
Red and yellow flowers
And she is telling me what to write.
"*You're* my muse?" I ask aghast.
"Why not, you shit. And now I quit!"

Progress Report

I stood at the crossroads;
Well, it was more an asterisk, really,
And I looked both ways,
Then up and down.

Then I about-faced quickly and repeated my liftings and
    turning.
Then I about-faced again and repeated again those same
Twistings and turnings.

When I feel it is alright to cross,
And figure out which direction to cross toward
I shall move forward.
Meanwhile,
I about-faced one more time.

Stadium

He touches the gut of his racket
With the energetic white ball and serves.

A big day at Forest Hills.

Tennis courts surrounded by ivy-grown Romanesque wall.

There is so much extra traffic in the sunny streets
And such smiles on the faces of the House of Harms
(Elsie, Gus, Herman, Kurt).
I am with my father in the press box.
His fingers daintily touching his "bug," he is relaxed,
    working.
I twist my head left to right, right to left to watch the game,
Not really liking it, but very glad to be here.
A child's misery doesn't last forever,
But it lasts much longer than his happiness.

The Day

The churches and temples were not
As thronged as one would have thought.
Bars and restaurants were doing nicely,
But nothing to write home about.

Woodstock's pagans
Were beginning to gather
'Round bonfires on Overlook Mountain.

Some of the poets preferred Shiv's back yard,
Smoking up their weed and savoring the moment.
Others decided to take in the end of the world
In the guise of a sort of Superbowl Sunday,
Around their television sets
With nachos and cold beer.

I turned down a number of invitations,
Electing instead to stay at home,
As I knew we would have done
Were you still alive.

We would have held hands
Like children. You would have said something like
"I'm glad you're here," and I would have replied
"Me too."

But you've been gone over ten years now,
So I'll just light a memorial candle and wait.

Man's Grandeur

How grand my species is!
And how perceptive
Of it to have invented tragedy!

Abandonment

The last rose of Sharon,
The only blossom this summer,
its forbears once so numerous
After Enid planted
Those four shrubs.

But I permitted
Their strangulation.

Now there is but one
Rose of Sharon blossom
To open gates to late summer's
Wide, wild thickness
Alive with weeds and crickets,
Deserving autumn's discipline
And winter's doom.

In Memoriam

The light she loved...
Of late afternoon...

Still touches worlds
    With gold

Apples

Apples piled in a stable,
The horses gone;

Left in panic
To enter fire

Or pull the sun.

The apples are brought
Into the cider house

Where a lecture
Is going on

On the meaning of autumn.

Let's Take A Look

Let's take a look
And maybe a photograph
Using of course my
Handy magical cell phone
Which is empowered to

Draw everything into a
Visual square

In which we can, by
Squinting correctly
Behold everything.
Murders riddle the back
Ground, while my
Personal ego swoops
Into the center of things
In a wonderful closeup.

I rather fancy the effect.
While I am witnessing and
Even photographically preserving
For all posterity the disgrace
And debacle that is the human
Experiment on this planet,
I am looking rather good for my age.
I only wish I had someone to send
A snapshot home to.

Good King Ludwig
For R. Dionysius Whiteurs, and remembering Robert Peters

Good King Ludwig of Bavaria
Was just finishing having his feet washed
Perhaps for the very last time
When a frown marched down his brow.

He could not at that moment imagine
Anything worthy a frown
Of his.

Cream.

He decreed Cream.
Now and forever:
Cream.

Definition

I'm trying to sleep off a drunk
In San Francisco when a light
Shines into my eyes.

In his other hand the cop
Holds a revolver, which I
Make a grab for.

That I am here, over
Half a century later
Recalling this

Is what is
Defined as
"White skin privilege."

Götterdämmerung

The *götterdämmerung*
Enveloping us
Deserves better than I can give.

I will rise on trembling pins,
Confront the insulting sun,
And open my mouth and utter
The usual blather.

I'll swallow some warm tea
Then make myself
A sandwich for breakfast.

Poem In Late October

The light's disappearing faster now
In more ways than one.

I'll leave the enumeration
To anyone who wants to do it.
Anybody can.

Author's Bio

Donald Lev, *b. 1936,* lives in High Falls, NY, where he continues to publish *Home Planet News*, the newsprint literary review he and his late wife, the poet Enid Dame, founded in 1979. He attended Hunter College and has worked in the wire rooms of the *Daily News* and the *New York Times*. He has been a literary activist in the New York area for decades. Lev hosted WNYC radio's "Open Poetry" program and has coordinated poetry readings at The Cedar Tavern in Greenwich Village, the Cafe Bookstore in Park Slope, The Day of the Poet in Stone Ridge, and at other venues too numerous to mention. He is the author of eleven collections of poetry, most recently *A Very Funny Fellow* (NYQ Books, 2012).

Also available from Presa Press

John Amen
At the Threshold of Alchemy
Kirby Congdon
Selected Poems & Prose Poems
Kirby Congdon - 65 Years of Poetry
Remarks and Reflections - Essays
Hugh Fox
Blood Cocoon - Selected Poems of Connie Fox
Eric Greinke
For The Living Dead - New & Selected Poems
The Potential Of Poetry
Ruth Moon Kempher
retrievals
Kerry Shawn Keys
Transporting, A Cloak of Rhapsodies
Lyn Lifshin
In Mirrors
Gerald Locklin
Deep Meanings: Selected Poems 2008-2013
Peter Ludwin
Rumors of Fallible Gods
Glenna Luschei
Witch Dance
Leaving It All Behind
Gary Metras
The Moon in the Pool
Stanley Nelson
Limbos For Amplified Harpsichord
City Of The Sun
Steven Sher
Grazing On Stars - Selected Poems
t. kilgore splake
splake fishing in america
winter river flowing selected poems 1979-2914
Alison Stone
Dangerous Enough
A.D. Winans
The Other Side of Broadway - Selected Poems
This Land Is Not My Land

See www.presapress.com for additional title information.